CYBER CRIME SECRETS

John Townsend

W

FRANKLIN WATTS

LONDON • SYDNEY

An Appleseed Editions book

First published in 2011 by Franklin Watts

Franklin Watts
338 Euston Road, London NW1 3BH

Franklin Watts Australia
Level 17/207 Kent St, Sydney, NSW 2000

© 2011 Appleseed Editions

Appleseed Editions Ltd
Well House, Friars Hill, Guestling, East Sussex TN35 4ET

Created by Q2AMedia
Editor: Katie Dicker
Art Director: Harleen Mehta
Designer: Cheena Yadav
Picture Researcher: Debabrata Sen

ISBN 978-1-4451-0389-1

Dewey classification: 364.1'68

All words in **bold** can be found in the Glossary on pages 30–31.

Website information is correct at the time of going to press. However, the publishers cannot
accept liability for any information or links found on third-party websites.

A CIP catalogue for this book is available from the British Library.

Picture credits
t= top, b= bottom, l= left, r= right
Cover images: ImageTeam/Shutterstock, Rich Legg/Istockphoto, Paul/Photolibrary.

Mikkel William Nielsen/Istockphoto: Title page, Rich Legg/Istockphoto: 4, Toria/Shutterstock: 5, Federico Ciamei/Istockphoto:
6, Carsten Reisinger/Dreamstime: 7, Jon Riley/Stone/Getty Images: 8, Rannev/Shutterstock: 9t, Ho New/Reuters, Joseph/
Shutterstock, Vladm/Shutterstock: 9, Edhar/Shutterstock: 10, Picture Perfect/Rex Features: 11, Chris Gramly/Istockphoto: 12,
Arest/Shutterstock: 13t, Pejo/Shutterstock: 13b, Mikkel William Nielsen/Istockphoto: 14, Slavoljub Pantelic/Shutterstock:
15t, Luis Louro/Shutterstock: 15b, Chris Jackson/Getty Images: 16, ImageTeam/Shutterstock: 17, Patti Sapone/AP Images: 18,
Jonathan Crellin: 19, Joroma/Shutterstock: 20, India Today Group/Getty Images: 21, Philippe Psaila/Science Photo Library:
22, Nikhil Gangavane/ Dreamstime: 23, Getty Images News/Getty Images: 24, Handout/Getty images News/Getty Images: 25,
Anyka/Shutterstock: 26, Jose Antonio Sanchez Reyes/Dreamstime: 27, Izabela Zaremba/Shutterstock: 28, David Hernandez/
Dreamstime: 29, ImageTeam/Shutterstock: 31.

Printed in Singapore

Franklin Watts is a division of Hachette Children's Books,
an Hachette Livre UK company.
www.hachettelivre.co.uk

CONTENTS

The digital age

Modern **forensic** science often involves far more than testing physical **evidence** found at a crime scene. It can include 'cyber evidence' – which is unseen electronic data and digital information.

Crime waves

A crime scene is anywhere a crime has been committed. This may be an obvious place, such as a smashed safe or an abandoned getaway car. But cyber crime is very different. This type of crime involves computers, mobile phones or other electronic equipment, and can take place anywhere.

Since the 1970s, the growth in technology has brought great advances to everyday life, but also to the world of crime. Today, some crime scene investigators specialise in **digital forensics**. They trace all kinds of instant messaging and computer-related communications.

A computer may be a crime scene, but its effects spread much further.

Growing threats

Cyber crime continues to grow every year, costing huge amounts of money. The USA's Federal Bureau of Investigation (FBI) has a 'cyber mission' to tackle:

- serious computer **hacking** and the spread of computer viruses (see page 6)
- Internet **fraud**
- online '**predators**'
- actions that affect national security.

Although computers have become major tools for today's criminals, cyber technology also has the power to catch many of these criminals at their own game. This book helps you to find out some amazing cyber crime secrets...

SCIENCE SECRETS

Cyber forensic scientists can extract the memory from laptop computers and mobile phones for crime scene evidence. A criminal's secret 'call history' can reveal details and dates of text messages, emails, images and videos. This information can be used as evidence in **court**.

Computers have brought more crime to the world, but they also help to catch criminals.

Cyber vandals

A vandal is someone who damages property. This is a criminal offence in most cases. Cyber vandals deliberately damage computers, by spreading computer viruses or faulty software.

Computer hackers damage the software on a computer.

Serious assault

Cyber vandals usually hack into websites and damage them just for fun. They get a buzz from proving they can break in and disrupt information. These attacks may seem fairly harmless, but the effect on some businesses can be serious. A damaged website has to be shut down and repaired before it can be used again. If vandals post racial, political or **obscene** messages on a website, it may become a crime scene.

Computer viruses

A computer virus is a type of **malware**. This software spreads via the Internet and infects computers through emails or corrupted weblinks. The virus 'infects' programs that change how a computer works, causing damage.

Other forms of computer vandalism include:

Worms – computer programs that copy themselves and spread through computer networks and the Internet.

Trojans – computer programs that claim to do one thing but really do another. They may damage a computer's hard drive or allow a hacker to access a computer system.

Spyware – computer programs that spy on what a user does with his or her computer, maybe revealing secret login codes or passwords.

Finding a virus on your computer is bad news.

Cyber criminal

In 2005, 17-year-old Sven Jaschan of Germany was given a 21-month **suspended sentence** after being found guilty of cyber vandalism. He had created the Sasser worm, which crippled computers around the world. He was lucky that he was too young to be sent to prison.

Cyber theft

Unlike cyber vandals, cyber thieves try to get rich – by hacking into computers to steal money or secrets to sell. Some cyber thieves have been teenagers robbing banks from their own bedrooms!

Stealing from home

Cyber thieves have been known to hack into a bank system to transfer money to their own account before withdrawing the stolen money. Others have hacked into a bank's security files to find account numbers, passwords and **PINs**. Sometimes, businesses will try to hack into a rival company to steal plans, secrets or even to adjust their accounts.

Cyber thieves often work undetected.

CASE FILE

In 2007, the mastermind behind a £10 million cyber theft was an 18-year-old computer whizzkid from New Zealand. 'AKILL', as he called himself, spent hours on his home computer every night to write software allowing criminals to access millions of bank accounts. The FBI eventually traced his criminal activities and arrested him.

CAN YOU BELIEVE IT?

Raphael Gray from Wales was just 19 when he hacked the credit card details of Microsoft founder Bill Gates in 2001. Three years earlier, a 16-year-old and a 17-year-old in California, USA, were caught hacking into the computer system at the **Pentagon**.

CASE FILE

In 2010, 28-year-old Albert Gonzalez was jailed for 20 years for cyber theft. As a teenager in Florida, USA, he used a school computer to hack into the government of India's computer system. But it was hacking into major US businesses that led to his conviction.

Gonzalez is now serving 20 years in prison.

Gonzalez sold millions of customers' account details to other criminals for an estimated US$2.8 million, which he used to buy an apartment, a car, Rolex watches and a US$75,000 birthday party. He also buried US$1 million cash in his parents' backyard. Gonzalez said he had become addicted to hacking. This highest earning hacker in history will now have to find other pastimes in prison.

Spam scam

Many cyber criminals send emails to trick people into revealing private information, such as bank card details. These scams, called **phishing**, allow thieves to make **illegal** purchases online.

Email scams

If an email directs you to a website where you are asked to give your personal details – beware! The website is likely to look real but it is probably a fake – set up to steal a user's information. Although 'cyber detectives' are always on the lookout for such scams and regularly catch the criminals, this type of fraud is on the increase.

You should beware of websites that ask for your personal details. They may be a hoax!

Junk mail

Spammers send out over 100 million junk emails a day. Many of these emails ask people to click on the links that make phishing attacks a multi-million pound industry. Criminals try to get victims to download harmful software onto their computers to steal bank account details and passwords.

Of the email messages sent in 2009, 87 per cent were spam emails. The death of Michael Jackson in that year generated the most spam – almost 2 per cent of all spam messages.

DID YOU KNOW?

Most spam emails come from the USA, where 60 per cent of all spam is created. China is the next largest generator of spam. However, scams and fraud only account for about 2 per cent of spam email. About 36 per cent of junk email is advertising.

Michael Jackson's death in 2009 created a new wave of spam emails.

World Cup tricks

Football fans were caught out by cyber criminals in the run-up to the 2010 Football World Cup with a series of spam emails, fake offers and attempts to steal bank account details. Anyone tricked into sending money received nothing in return.

Identity theft

A lot of cyber crime involves stealing people's personal details for illegal use, for entering a country, or even causing acts of terrorism. Such identity theft lets a criminal pretend to be someone else.

Growing crime

According to experts, another person becomes a victim of online identity theft every 79 seconds. That means many millions of people have already had their private details stolen and used by criminals for illegal purposes. The following two cases from 2008 show how digital forensics caught out identity thieves.

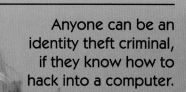

Anyone can be an identity theft criminal, if they know how to hack into a computer.

DID YOU KNOW?

Bots are now often used by cyber criminals. They allow hackers to take control of many computers at a time and turn them into 'zombie' computers. These operate as part of a 'botnet' to spread viruses, generate spam, and commit other types of online crime and fraud.

CASE FILE

In 2008, a 16-year-old boy known only as Ajay became an identity thief in Ahmedabad, India. He hacked into websites and stole customers' numbers and personal details to sell to other criminals. Ajay's tools were his laptop computer and a mobile phone. He was very careful to cover his tracks, leaving no digital evidence on his own computer. However, the evidence against him came from another gang member who left **incriminating** details on his own computer. Once arrested, Ajay showed the police a few of his tricks and helped them to track down other identity thieves.

A computer fraud can take place in a teenager's bedroom!

CASE FILE

Bonnie and Clyde were famous bank robbers in the USA in the 1930s. In 2008, another US couple became known as the 'Bonnie and Clyde' of identity fraud. Edward Anderton (aged 26) and Jocelyn Kirsch (aged 23) stole personal information from friends, colleagues and neighbours to pay for an extravagant lifestyle. The couple stole about US$120,000 from their victims before their computer equipment was seized. Anderton was sent to prison for four years, while Kirsch received a five-year sentence because she continued her crimes after being questioned by the police.

Terrorism

Cyber terrorism involves criminal activities that target national security data. This type of terrorism attacks computer systems and accesses top-secret information to cause fear and violence.

Growing threats

Cyber terrorism is a rapidly expanding threat. But cyber terrorists have sometimes been caught and convicted because of information stored on their own computers.

CAN YOU BELIEVE IT?

John Allen Muhammad was executed by lethal injection in 2009 for a string of shootings that terrorised Washington DC, USA, in 2002. A laptop computer in his car helped cyber forensics to trace his steps. The computer contained key evidence such as a **ransom** note demanding US$5 million, code words and a map of his crime scenes.

Cyber terrorists use their hacking skills to cause fear and violence in different countries of the world.

CASE FILE

In 2007, Michael Curtis Reynolds of Montana, USA, was convicted of cyber terrorist activities. He had used the Internet to involve **Al-Qaeda** in a plot to blow up the Trans-Continental gas pipeline, a Wyoming oil refinery and the Trans-Alaska oil pipeline. The FBI gathered evidence from his computers and emails which outlined his bomb plans.

Reynolds was arrested by the FBI in 2005, while trying to collect a bag filled with US$40,000. He thought the money was being supplied by an Al-Qaeda contact he met online. During his trial, Reynolds claimed that he was trying to catch terrorists on the Internet to report them to the FBI. But digital evidence proved Reynolds had supplied details of bomb-making equipment for terrorist attacks. He was sentenced to 30 years in prison.

Cyber terrorism is a growing threat, so forensic experts keep track of digital evidence.

Cyber forensics

CSI officers often look for a **suspect's** computer so that experts can test it for secrets, including deleted information. Usually they need a **warrant** to search someone's personal property.

The search for clues

Like any investigation, a seized computer must be made secure so no digital information is altered or lost. Computer experts look for files that are **encrypted**, protected by passwords, hidden or deleted. The files are copied, so the original data remains unchanged, and records are kept to ensure that accurate evidence is used in court.

When a computer is seized, it is wrapped in plastic to preserve fingerprints and other evidence.

Chat room danger

Making friends using online chat rooms can be risky because you never know who you are talking to. Ashleigh Hall, a 17-year-old student from Darlington, UK, agreed to meet a young 'friend' she had met online. He turned out to be Peter Chapman, a 33-year-old predator. He strangled Ashleigh and left her body in a field.

When digital forensic experts examined Ashleigh's computer, they found Peter Chapman's false identity on the social networking site Facebook. The police arrested him and he was sentenced to life in prison in 2010.

Forensic scientists can find many secrets when they examine the inside of a computer.

DID YOU KNOW?

Some criminals make it more difficult for investigators to find information on their hard drives, by using programs known as anti-forensics. Detectives have to disable these programs to get to the hidden information they need. But with the right software, they can even find long-deleted files.

Clues to a murder

A particularly gruesome killing made headline news in the USA, in 2007, when a woman went on trial for the murder of her husband. It was mainly computer evidence that sent Melanie McGuire to prison.

Grim discovery

In May 2004, a fisherman pulled a suitcase from the sea in Chesapeake Bay, Maryland, USA. He was horrified to find human body parts inside. A week later two more suitcases containing body parts were washed up on a nearby beach. CSI officers were soon trying to find out who the victim was. He had been shot before his body was cut up.

Within weeks, detectives knew the name of the victim. William McGuire was identified when a sketch of his face was published and recognised by William's friend. Very soon, William's wife Melanie became the chief suspect in his murder.

Melanie McGuire, aged 34, was put on trial for the murder of her husband William in 2004.

Vital evidence

Forensic scientists began linking William's death to the family home in Woodbridge, New Jersey, which they believed to be the murder scene:

- Plastic bags in which the murderer placed William McGuire's body parts were similar to bags found in the McGuire home.

- The suitcases in which William McGuire's body parts were found were shown to belong to the McGuires.

- Melanie McGuire had bought a drug from a local pharmacy just before her husband went missing.

Cyber clues

However, it was the evidence found on Melanie's computer that suggested she drugged her husband before shooting him and disposing of his body. Computer data showed Internet searches for information on drugs, guns and poisons. Melanie McGuire was sentenced to life in prison.

Computer hard drives containing tell-tale evidence are examined by cyber experts to find hidden information – even deleted data.

CAN YOU BELIEVE IT?

Melanie McGuire could not hide the secrets on her computer. Shortly before her husband's murder, searches had included 'how to commit murder', 'how to purchase guns', and 'undetectable poisons'. One search related to the pharmacy where, on the morning of the murder, she purchased a drug using a false name.

Sat-nav spies

Any criminal using a **GPS device** to help find or escape from a crime scene is storing digital evidence. This information can help forensic detectives to trace a criminal's steps.

Hidden secrets

Drivers who use sat-navs (satellite navigation) may not realise they have a spy in their vehicle. Digital information stored on the memory card can reveal where the driver was at a particular time. Details of a suspect's whereabouts at different times, each journey, and addresses of contacts can all be recovered from GPS equipment. The police may find this information very useful!

DID YOU KNOW?

Digital devices known as 'event data recorders' are now standard equipment in many new cars. They record speed, braking, signalling or other driving behaviour and can show forensic investigators vital details about a crime, a crash, or getaway car chases.

The sat-nav system in a car can hold many vital clues to a person's daily journeys.

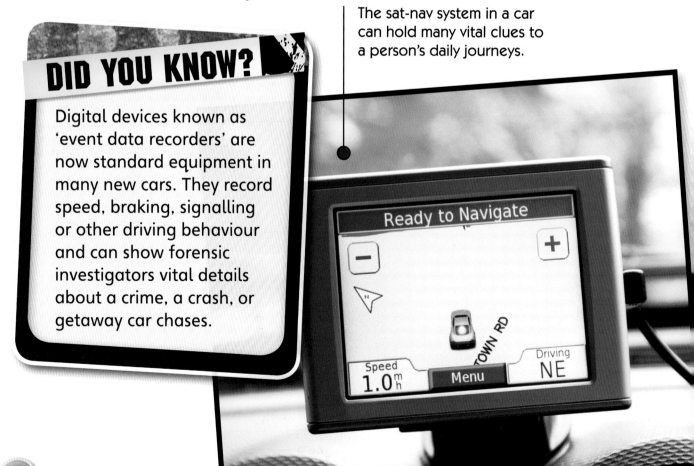

Ready to Navigate

Speed
1.0 m/h

Menu

Driving
NE

CASE FILE

When terrorists attacked the Taj Mahal Palace hotel in Mumbai, India, in 2008, they killed more than 170 people with guns and grenades. After a terrifying gun battle, nine of the terrorist gunmen were killed.

A mobile phone and three GPS devices found inside their abandoned vehicles after the attacks proved to forensic experts that ten terrorists had set out from the Pakistani city of Karachi. As nine of them had been killed, the tenth man faced charges of terrorism, murder and possessing explosives.

This terrorist was 22-year-old Mohammad Ajmal Amir Qasab of Pakistan. The digital evidence from his sat-nav helped the police to gather information about addresses and the routes he had taken. At first Qasab pleaded not guilty, but later confessed that he was one of the gunmen. In 2010, he was convicted of his crimes and sentenced to death.

Fire and smoke poured from the hotel as troops and terrorists carried out a gun battle.

Mobile phone secrets

Your mobile phone hides many secrets about you. It can trace your movements and even tell forensic scientists if you are a criminal!

The spy in your pocket

Memory cards in mobile phones are packed with information – from contact lists and messages (including deleted text), to call-logs and data about where the phone has been used. These details can uncover a criminal's recent history.

DID YOU KNOW?

To catch criminals from digital evidence, cyber forensic researchers have designed a device called a flasher box. This transfers data from a mobile phone to a computer. It helps detectives without any electronic expertise to check for digital clues, when trying to solve criminal cases.

The data from a mobile phone can be downloaded onto a computer in seconds, to reveal vital clues.

CASE FILE

Joe O'Reilly was convicted in 2007 of murdering his wife Rachel at their home in Dublin, Ireland. Much of the evidence against him came from his mobile phone. From his calls, the police were able to plot exactly where O'Reilly was around the time of his wife's murder. Each time a mobile phone is used, it connects to a cell on a mast that serves a specific area. This precise information gets recorded inside the phone.

Rachel O'Reilly's badly beaten body was found in 2004. Her husband, aged 35, was eventually jailed for life because of the digital evidence inside his phone.

Text evidence

If you think text messages can be anonymous, think again! Experts can study every detail in a text or email to discover who sent it.

In 2005, 19-year-old Jenny Nicholl from Yorkshire, UK, went missing and was never seen again. David Hodgson (aged 48) had killed her, but to make her family think she was still alive, he texted them from Jenny's phone. Forensic **linguists** proved the text messages were not from Jenny but instead matched the style of Hodgson, a suspect. In 2008, Hodgson was sent to prison for Jenny's murder.

The style of a text message can give clues to the sender's identity.

Mobile evidence

Two murder cases in the UK at the start of the millennium were particularly shocking because the victims were ten-year-old children. Mobile phone evidence was used in both trials.

Schoolboy attack

In 2000, Damilola Taylor was found bleeding to death in a stairway to flats in Peckham, London. Forensic scientists believed he had been attacked, before falling on a broken bottle. Damilola later died from his wounds. Whoever would attack a ten-year-old on his way home from school?

Two years later, two 16-year-old brothers went on trial for Damilola's murder, but mobile phone evidence cleared them of the crime. The judge ruled they could not have killed Damilola because their phones had been used too far from the crime scene at the time. It was another four years before the youths responsible for Damilola's death were convicted.

The death of Damilola Taylor led to a massive police hunt for his killers.

Missing girls

In 2002, Holly Wells and Jessica Chapman went out to buy sweets in their home town of Soham near Cambridge, UK. They walked past the school caretaker's house where 36-year-old Ian Huntley lived. He invited the girls inside, where he killed them before hiding their bodies a few miles away.

Local people, including Huntley, helped the police to search for the missing girls. Mobile phone evidence then made the police look more closely at Huntley. Digital forensics showed exactly where and when Jessica's last phone signal had been switched off. It was linked to a mobile phone mast near to the caretaker's house. Ian Huntley was eventually convicted of the girls' murder from a variety of evidence and sent to prison for life.

Holly Wells (left) and her best friend Jessica Chapman were tragically murdered in 2002.

SCIENCE SECRETS

Some forensic scientists warn that, although computers and mobile phones can hold all kinds of useful digital evidence, it is not always foolproof. After all, a criminal might get someone else to use his phone while he's robbing a bank, just to give himself an **alibi**!

Catching criminals

Computer forensic laboratories across the USA examine thousands of electrical devices every year in the search for criminal evidence. There can be many surprises.

Will these flames destroy the evidence on this hard drive?

Guilty secrets

FBI files contain bizarre stories of desperate people trying to destroy digital evidence that might get them into trouble. One report told of a suspect who tried to burn down his own house, hoping the flames would destroy his computer hard drive, which held enough evidence to send him to prison. But he failed.

Another man shot a bullet through his computer in an attempt to destroy the hard drive – which he did. However, a second hard drive was full of incriminating evidence, so he went to prison after all. Throwing computers and mobile phones into rivers rarely works, either. Data is usually waterproof!

CASE FILE

An armed gang robbed 21 banks in Texas, USA, before the FBI caught the five robbers in 2008. Known as the 'Scarecrow Bandits', the robbers all wore floppy hats and flannel shirts as a form of disguise.

At their trial, mobile phone records, recorded conversations and images from aerial **surveillance** teams were presented as evidence. Digital forensics experts used text messages, photographs and call-logs from the gang's 14 phones to convict the men.

One of the phones was recovered from a sewer after being there for two days – after a suspect tried to flush it down a toilet. Each gang member received a long prison sentence, with the leader being sent to prison for 354 years!

DID YOU KNOW?

Once a sealed mobile phone or computer arrives at a secure lab, it is given to a forensic examiner to uncover the data. Video images of crime scenes may also arrive for examination. The latest software can gather a lot of useful information from images recorded on **CCTV** cameras.

Forensic scientists can work out when and where a victim's body fell in the water from the moment their mobile phone stopped working.

What next?

Cyber crime secrets will become even more amazing as technology continues to develop. Cyber criminals and cyber forensics will each try to keep one step ahead in the 'cyber crime race'.

Cyber spies

Just one area where computer scientists are developing new software and high-tech equipment in the fight against crime is the latest digital CCTV. Cameras pointing at us in busy airports or stations will soon do far more than record fuzzy pictures. New technology will do forensic work 'live' by instantly assessing threats and warning of crimes about to take place.

CCTV digital technology is always watching us!

Warning signs

What is now called 'Intelligent CCTV' can detect unusual situations or recognise a suspect in a crowd. This 'computer vision technology' can check for patterns of behaviour that may go undetected by the human eye. If anyone is acting strangely, a computer can assess the situation and if there seems to be a major risk, the police are alerted.

Matching faces

The latest high-definition digital CCTV cameras could be used to identify criminals even if they have changed their appearance. Face-recognition technology scans an image of a suspect's face and records accurate measurements, such as the distance between the eyes. This 'face data' can quickly find a match on a database of known criminals. Whatever the future holds, it seems certain that forensic experts will be looking at us more closely...

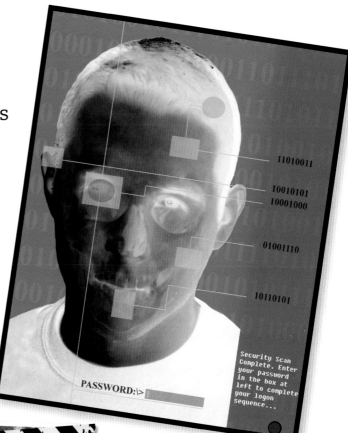

A computer scan of a suspect's face can be matched against police records.

SCIENCE SECRETS

Intelligent CCTV will soon be listening, too! Computer scientists are developing audio-recognition software to listen for particular sounds, such as screams. The camera will instantly swivel to the direction of the sound and analyse a high definition image in milliseconds.

Glossary

alibi
proof that someone accused of a crime was at another place during the crime

Al-Qaeda
an organisation behind some global terrorist attacks, such as those targeting the USA on 11 Sept 2001

bot
short for robot – this is a computer program that allows an attacker to gain control over affected computers

CCTV
closed-circuit television

court
the place where a criminal is questioned and proven innocent or guilty

CSI
crime scene investigation

digital forensics
the collection and presentation of digitally-stored evidence in criminal investigations

encrypted
concealed information by means of a code

evidence
material presented to a court in a crime case

firewall
computer software that prevents access by unauthorised users

forensic
using scientific methods to investigate and establish facts in criminal courts

fraud
using dishonest methods to cheat another person of something valuable

GPS device
a global positioning system device that uses satellites to locate a moving vehicle or person

hacking
gaining access to a computer illegally

illegal
against the law

incriminating
to show evidence or proof of involvement in a crime

linguist
a language specialist

malware
'malicious software' programs designed to damage a computer system

obscene
very shocking
and offensive

Pentagon
the main building
of the US defence
department in
Washington, USA

phishing
to send trick
emails with links
to fake website
pages to fool users
into giving their
personal details

PIN
personal
identification
number

predator
someone who
bullies, victimises
or preys on another

ransom
something paid
or demanded for
the freedom of a
captured person

spammer
someone who sends
unwanted emails
to a large number
of email addresses

spyware
technology that
helps to find
information about
people without
their knowledge

surveillance
keeping a
close watch

suspect
someone thought
to be guilty of
a crime

suspended sentence
a prison sentence
that does not take
effect immediately
unless the criminal
offends again

trojan
a seemingly useful
computer program
that contains
instructions to
cause damage

warrant
a legal document
giving a police officer
the power to carry
out the law

worm
a harmful computer
program that sends
copies of itself
to attack other
computers on
a network

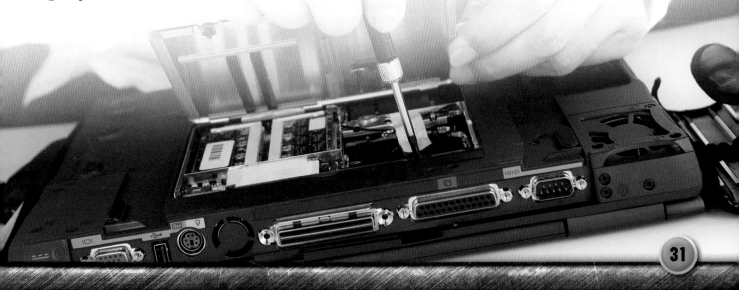

Index

Webfinder

http://computer.howstuffworks.com/worst-computer-viruses.htm
Learn about some of the worst computer viruses of all time.

http://computer.howstuffworks.com/computer-forensic.htm
Discover more about the use of computer forensics in the hunt for criminals.

http://investigation.discovery.com/videos/solved-computer-forensics.html
This short film looks at how computer forensics helped to convict Melanie McGuire.

http://investigation.discovery.com/videos/solved-cell-phone-tracking.html
This short film looks at how mobile phone evidence can help to trace a killer.

www.mcgruffspo.com/cybersafetysat.cfm
Use this poster to help protect yourself and others from cyber crime.